Profiles of the Presidents

MILLARD
FILLMORE

★ ★ ★

Profiles of the Presidents

MILLARD FILLMORE

by Andrew Santella

Content Adviser: Harry Rubenstein, Curator of Political History Collections, National Museum of American History, Smithsonian Institution

Reading Adviser: Dr. Linda D. Labbo, Department of Reading Education, College of Education, The University of Georgia

COMPASS POINT BOOKS ✦ MINNEAPOLIS, MINNESOTA

Compass Point Books
3109 West 50th Street, #115
Minneapolis, MN 55410

Visit Compass Point Books on the Internet at *www.compasspointbooks.com*
or e-mail your request to *custserv@compasspointbooks.com*

Photographs ©: White House Collection, Courtesy White House Historical Association (38), cover, 3; Library of Congress, 6, 17, 28, 30, 33 (bottom), 36, 48 (left), 57 (right), 58 (left), 59 (left); Lombard Antiquarian Maps & Prints, 7, 14, 27, 56 (left), 57 (left); Stock Montage, 8, 41, 58 (bottom left); North Wind Picture Archives, 10, 19, 22, 24, 29, 31, 33 (top), 35, 42, 43, 49, 58 (top left); Buffalo and Erie County Historical Society, 11, 12, 15, 16, 21, 37, 48 (right), 54 (left), 55 (left); Bettmann/Corbis, 13, 18; Hulton/Archive by Getty Images, 20, 25, 26, 34, 39, 40, 45, 47, 54 (right), 55 (top right), 56 (right), 57 (bottom right), 59 (top right); National Portrait Gallery, Smithsonian Institution/Art Resource, N.Y., 23; Photographed by Erik Kvalsvik for White House Historical Association (1022), 38; David J. & Janice L. Frent Collection/Corbis, 46; Courtesy of Forest Lawn Cemetery, Buffalo, New York, 50; Department of Rare Books and Special Collections, University of Rochester Library, 55 (bottom right); Texas State Library & Archives Commission, 57 (top right); Bruce Burkhardt/Corbis, 57 (middle right); Union Pacific Museum Collection, 59 (bottom right).

Editors: E. Russell Primm, Emily J. Dolbear, Melissa McDaniel, and Catherine Neitge
Photo Researcher: Svetlana Zhurkina
Photo Selector: Linda S. Koutris
Designer/Page Production: The Design Lab/Les Tranby
Cartographer: XNR Productions, Inc.

Library of Congress Cataloging-in-Publication Data
Santella, Andrew.
    Millard Fillmore / by Andrew Santella.
        p. cm.—(Profiles of the presidents)
Summary: A biography of the thirteenth president of the United States, discussing his personal life, education, and political career.
Includes bibliographical references (p.) and index.
    ISBN 0-7565-0261-6 (alk. paper)
    1. Fillmore, Millard, 1800–1874—Juvenile literature. 2. Presidents—United States—Biography—Juvenile literature. [1. Fillmore, Millard, 1800–1874. 2. Presidents.] I. Title. II. Series.
    E427 .S26 2003
    973.6'4'092—dc21   2002153521

Table of Contents

★   ★   ★

*NOTE: In this book, words that are defined in the glossary are in **bold** the first time they appear in the text.*

Anger in the Senate

★ ★ ★

Members of the U.S. Senate are supposed to have lively and spirited **debates.** On April 17, 1850, however, the debate on the floor of the Senate was a little too

Senator Henry S. Foote

spirited. For weeks, Senator Henry S. Foote of Mississippi had been making speeches criticizing Senator Thomas Hart Benton of Missouri. Some of Foote's speeches insulted Benton. In one speech, Foote even suggested that Benton was a coward.

◀ *As vice president,
Millard Fillmore was
presiding officer of
the Senate.*

To make Foote stop his insults, Benton turned to the man in charge of the Senate. That man's name was Millard Fillmore. As vice president of the United States, Fillmore had the duty of **presiding** over the Senate.

Senator Thomas ▶
Hart Benton turned
to Millard Fillmore to
end Foote's insults
on the Senate floor.

Fillmore reminded Foote and the rest of the senators to keep order. Foote did not. Instead, he flung more insults Benton's way.

Benton had heard enough. He rose from his chair and headed toward Foote. Foote backed away and pulled a pistol from his coat pocket. Senators jumped to their feet to come between the two men. Benton dared Foote to shoot him, spreading his arms to make a better target. Someone wrestled Foote's pistol away from him and hid it in a desk. Fillmore banged his **gavel** repeatedly to get everyone's attention. He called for order in the Senate chamber. "Senators will be seated," he demanded. "Business cannot proceed until order is restored."

Foote, Benton, and the rest of the senators eventually calmed down. Fillmore sent the senators home. Everyone left thankful that there had been no violence on the floor of the Senate.

What drove important political leaders to such shameful behavior? The heart of their argument was slavery. It was the biggest issue in American politics in the 1850s. At that time, Southern states allowed slavery, while Northern states banned it. People argued constantly over whether slavery would be allowed in the western lands that the United States had acquired.

As vice president and presiding officer of the Senate, Millard Fillmore was in the middle of the debate over slavery. He struggled to keep the arguments from spinning out of control, but he was not always successful.

Little did Fillmore know that soon he would be thrust even deeper into the debate. Fillmore would shortly become president of the United States. He would find that the argument over slavery was no easier to manage from the White House than it had been from the floor of the Senate.

Slaves going to ▼ work on a sugar plantation in the South

Early Life

★ ★ ★

Millard Fillmore was born into a life of hard work and poverty. His parents were Nathaniel and Phoebe Fillmore. They made their home in a tiny log cabin in Cayuga County, in upstate New York. The area was so sparsely settled that the Fillmores' nearest neighbors lived 4 miles (6 kilometers) away. On January 7, 1800, the Fillmores welcomed their first son into the world. They named him Millard, which was Phoebe's family name.

▼ *Nathaniel Fillmore*

The Fillmores already had a daughter named Olive. They eventually had eight children, and their small cabin became quite crowded. The Fillmores struggled just to keep the children fed and clothed. They had little success farming the rocky soil and finally had to give up their land. They moved a few miles south, to a small town now called Niles. There they began working as tenant farmers, which meant they worked land that was owned by someone else.

This photograph ▼ of five of the Fillmore children in 1843 shows (from left) Olive, Millard, Cyrus, Calvin, and Julia.

Millard learned early how hard a farmer's life can be. He helped his father plow fields, mow hay, clear land, and cut logs for firewood. As Millard grew up, he took on more and more responsibilities at home.

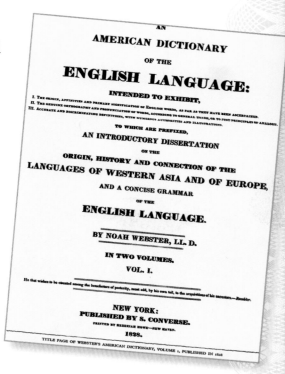

AN

AMERICAN DICTIONARY

OF THE

ENGLISH LANGUAGE:

INTENDED TO EXHIBIT,

I. THE ORIGIN, AFFINITIES AND PRIMARY SIGNIFICATION OF ENGLISH WORDS, AS FAR AS THEY HAVE BEEN ASCERTAINED.
II. THE GENUINE ORTHOGRAPHY AND PRONUNCIATION OF WORDS, ACCORDING TO GENERAL USAGE, OR TO JUST PRINCIPLES OF ANALOGY.
III. ACCURATE AND DISCRIMINATING DEFINITIONS, WITH NUMEROUS AUTHORITIES AND ILLUSTRATIONS.

TO WHICH ARE PREFIXED,

AN INTRODUCTORY DISSERTATION

ON THE

ORIGIN, HISTORY AND CONNECTION OF THE
LANGUAGES OF WESTERN ASIA AND OF EUROPE,

AND A CONCISE GRAMMAR

OF THE

ENGLISH LANGUAGE.

BY NOAH WEBSTER, LL. D.

IN TWO VOLUMES.
VOL. I.

He that wishes to be counted among the benefactors of posterity, must add, by his own toil, to the acquisitions of his ancestors.—Rambler.

NEW YORK:
PUBLISHED BY S. CONVERSE.
PRINTED BY HEZEKIAH HOWE—NEW HAVEN.
1828.

TITLE PAGE OF WEBSTER'S AMERICAN DICTIONARY, VOLUME 1, PUBLISHED IN 1828

▲ *The title page of a dictionary from the early 1800s*

Nathaniel Fillmore was determined that Millard would not have to spend his life farming. He wanted his son to learn a different line of work. When Millard turned fourteen, his father arranged for him to work with a cloth maker in Sparta, New York. Millard worked there for about a year, but he disliked his job so much that he left Sparta and walked the 100 miles (161 km) back home. He found another job with a cloth maker closer to home and worked there for two years.

As a boy, Millard had been so busy on the family farm that he did not get much formal schooling. Now Millard was eager to improve his education. According to one story, he used what little money he had earned to buy a dictionary. In his spare time, he paged

Abigail Powers ▲ was a teacher at New Hope Academy and met Millard Fillmore when he was a student there.

through the diction-
ary, teaching himself
new words.

When Fillmore
was eighteen, he
enrolled in New
Hope Academy.
There he learned
grammar and filled
in other gaps in his
education. More im-
portantly, he met
a teacher who would
change his life. Her
name was Abigail
Powers, and she was just two years older than Fillmore.
She saw that he wanted to learn, and she did her best to
help him. The two shared a love of books and knowledge.
Before long, they fell in love and became engaged.

Before they could marry, Fillmore had to find a way
to support a family. His father helped him get a job as
a law clerk for a judge. With the judge's help, Fillmore
began studying the law. He became a lawyer in 1823.

That year, Fillmore moved to East Aurora, a town near
Buffalo in western New York. He opened that town's first
law office. After two years, he had become one of East
Aurora's leading citizens. He was also earning a good living.
Now he could finally ask Abigail to marry him.

▲ *Fillmore's law office
in East Aurora*

★

On February, 5, 1826, the two were married. For the rest of her life, Abigail Fillmore would be Millard's most trusted adviser and his most loyal supporter. In time, they would have two children. Their son, Millard Powers Fillmore, was born in 1828. A daughter named Mary Abigail Fillmore followed in 1832.

Millard and Abigail ▼ Fillmore began a family in this home in East Aurora.

New York Politics

★ ★ ★

By the time of his marriage, Fillmore had become interested in politics. In 1826, he joined the Anti-Masonic
movement. Members of this political movement believed
that a secret society called the Masons held too much
power in America. Many of
America's political leaders
were Masons. Anti-Masons
wanted to drive Masons out
of positions of power. The
Anti-Masonic movement
got its start in the small
towns of upstate New
York. It soon spread to
other states in the North-
east. By 1828, the Anti-
Masons had become a
major political party in
the region.

▼ This Masonic poster
is critical of the Anti-
Masons political
party, to which
Fillmore belonged

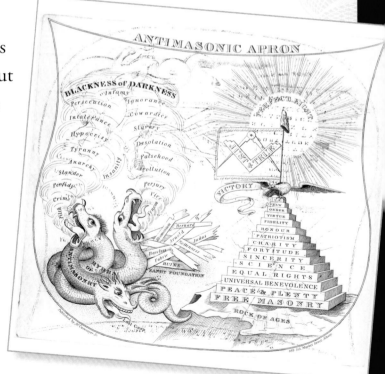

Fillmore during his time in the New York state legislature

In 1828, Fillmore ran for the New York state **legislature** as an Anti-Masonic **candidate.** Fillmore won and eventually served three terms in the state legislature. During that time, he helped pass two important state laws. The first law made it illegal to put people in jail for not being able to pay their debts. The second law helped small business owners keep their businesses running during difficult times.

Fillmore's law practice was also doing well. In 1830, he moved his family to the bustling city of Buffalo, New York. Buffalo was the biggest and busiest town Fillmore had ever lived in. He and Abigail quickly became part of Buffalo society. They joined groups that worked for better public education and an improved public library system in Buffalo. Their home became a meeting place for other ambitious young people. For a poor farmer's son, the busy life in Buffalo was quite a change. However, Fillmore's life would soon change even more dramatically.

Birth of a New Party

★ ★ ★

In 1832, Fillmore was elected to the U.S. Congress. For the first time, the young politician would be heading to the nation's capital to help make national laws.

Fillmore took his seat in the House of Representatives as a member of the Anti-Masonic Party. By the time he arrived in Washington in 1833, however, a new

▼ *Washington, D.C., in the 1830s*

national political party was beginning to form that was against the policies of President Andrew Jackson. At first, members of the new party called themselves the Anti-Jacksonians. They soon came to be known as the Whigs, a name they borrowed from a political party in England. By 1836, the Whig movement had spread across several states and had become a truly national party. Supporters of Jackson became known as the Democratic-Republicans, or simply the Democrats.

The Whig ▼ Party disagreed with many of the policies of President Andrew Jackson.

During Fillmore's first term in Congress, he often voted against President Jackson's policies. This made him a natural member of the Whig Party. However, Fillmore knew that he stood little chance of being elected to Congress as a Whig. The Whig Party was not yet popular back home in Buffalo. After a two-year term in Congress, Fillmore decided not to run for reelection.

Instead, he began trying to convince people in Buffalo to join the new Whig Party. At that time, newspaper articles explaining a party's beliefs were very helpful in gaining support for a political party. Fillmore arranged for an old friend named Dr. Thomas A. Foote to take over as editor of the Buffalo *Commercial Advertiser*. With

◀ The Commercial Advertiser *building in Buffalo*

Foote in charge, the newspaper became a solid supporter of Whig policies—and of Millard Fillmore.

Fillmore's work as a lawyer also helped him win supporters. In 1835, he did legal work to help protect people who owned small plots of land in western New York. Many of these landowners had a hard time paying off their debts under the unfair system set up by wealthy lenders.

Fillmore did legal work to protect landowners like these farmers on a grain boat on the Erie Canal in western New York.

Because of Fillmore's actions, more people in the Buffalo region began supporting the Whig Party. This enabled him to be elected to Congress as a Whig in 1836. He served three more terms, from 1837 to 1842. During that time, Fillmore became one of the leading members of the House of Representatives.

In 1842, Fillmore left Congress to return to his law practice in Buffalo. He did not drop out of politics, however. He continued to act as a leader of the

Whig Party in New York. In 1844, some Whigs wanted Fillmore to be their party's choice for vice president, but another man was ultimately chosen instead. Denied the chance to run for national office, Fillmore decided to run for governor of New York. He was disappointed in that contest, as well. Fillmore lost a close election to Democrat Silas Wright.

Thurlow Weed was one of the Whig leaders Fillmore blamed for his defeat when he ran for governor of New York.

Fillmore was deeply hurt by the defeat. "All is gone but honor," he said. He blamed Whig Party leaders Thurlow Weed and William Seward for not providing enough support during his **campaign** for governor.

By 1847, he was ready for another run at public office. This time he ran for the position of state **comptroller** of New York. It was not as glamorous as being

governor or senator, but the comptroller had real power over the state's finances. Fillmore easily won the election.

His big victory caught the attention of Whig leaders across the country. Just one year later, Fillmore would get his chance to run for national office.

▲ *Wall Street, New York's financial district, in the 1840s*

Vice President

★ ★ ★

When Fillmore became state comptroller of New York, the United States was already at war with Mexico. The war had begun in 1846 over a dispute about the border between Texas and Mexico. In 1847, U.S. troops captured the Mexican capital of Mexico City, and by 1848 the war

U.S. troops ▼
captured
Mexico City in
September 1847.

was over. As a result of the victory over Mexico, the United States took a huge stretch of territory in the Southwest. The United States gained the present-day states of New Mexico, Arizona, Utah, Nevada, and California, and parts of Wyoming and Colorado.

The U.S. victory created an important political question: Should slavery be allowed in these vast new territories? That question would be one of the main issues in the 1848 presidential election.

▲ *Zachary Taylor was a popular war hero and the Whig presidential candidate in the 1848 election.*

In June 1848, Whigs from all over the country gathered at their **convention** to choose candidates for president and vice president of the United States. For president, they turned to a hero from the Mexican War— General Zachary Taylor. He had led American troops to victory in key battles during the war. Taylor was one of the most popular men in the country.

Whigs nominated ▲
Millard Fillmore
as their vice
presidential
candidate in 1848.

However, the Whigs faced a problem in choosing a vice presidential candidate to run with Taylor. General Taylor was a Southerner from Louisiana who owned slaves. Some Whigs feared that he would scare away voters who were against slavery. Therefore, the Whigs decided to choose a Northerner as their vice presidential candidate. They settled on Millard Fillmore of New York.

Whig leaders liked Fillmore because he took the middle road on the question of slavery. He was from a Northern state and had never owned slaves, so he might win over voters who opposed slavery. He also made it clear that he had no desire to put an end to slavery where it already existed. That view pleased Southern slave owners. In the end, Fillmore was appealing to both Northern and Southern voters. He was also careful not to take any position on the difficult question of whether slavery should be allowed in new western territories. That way he wouldn't anger anyone.

Fillmore turned out to be a good choice for the Whigs. He campaigned hard on Taylor's behalf. In November 1848, Taylor won a close victory over the Democratic candidate, Senator Lewis Cass of Michigan. Fillmore had a new job—vice president of the United States.

Senator Lewis Cass lost the 1848 election to Zachary Taylor.

Taylor and Fillmore never worked together during the campaign. In fact, the two did not even meet each other until about a week before they were sworn in as

Though they campaigned on the same ticket, Taylor (left) and Fillmore had little in common.

president and vice president. The meeting did not go well. Their conversation was awkward. The two men found they had little in common. Even their physical appearances were different. Fillmore was tall and well-dressed; Taylor was short and a bit sloppy.

Taylor was busy getting ready to become president. He had to select his advisers and assistants. He had to think about what he would try to achieve as president. Fillmore could have helped him with these tasks. After all, Fillmore had more than twenty years of political experience—more than Taylor himself. However, Taylor never asked for his advice. It was not a good sign.

Taylor and Fillmore took office on March 5, 1849. It soon became clear that Taylor was not interested in Fillmore playing an important part in his presidency. Taylor didn't give his vice president much to do. Worse yet, Taylor often turned to Fillmore's rival, Senator William Seward of New York, for advice. Fillmore found himself with little to do except preside over the debates on the floor of the Senate.

▲ *Senator William Seward was Fillmore's political rival.*

Many of these debates had to do with the new territories in the West. Would slavery be permitted there or not? President Taylor wanted California and other territories to become states as quickly as possible. He proposed a plan that would allow the people of the western territories to decide for themselves about slavery. Everyone knew what

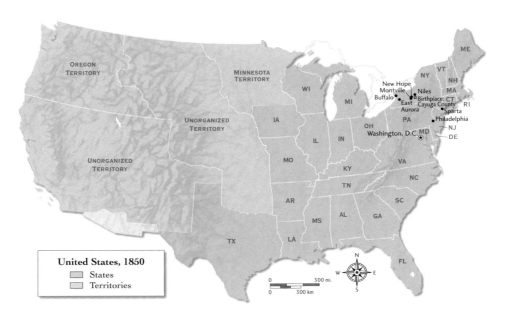

United States, 1850
States
Territories

the result of this plan would be: Two or three new states that banned slavery would enter the Union.

Southern leaders were outraged by Taylor's plan. They knew that it would destroy the balance between **free states** and **slave states.** At that time, the United States consisted of fifteen free states and fifteen slave states. Some Southerners threatened that their states would leave the Union if Taylor's plan went into effect.

Seventy-year-old senator Henry Clay of Kentucky suggested a **compromise.** California would join the Union as a free state. Other new western territories would decide for themselves whether to allow slavery or not. Buying and selling slaves would become illegal in Washington, D.C. To satisfy slavery's supporters, the compromise also included a harsh runaway slave law. Under the proposed law, escaped slaves captured anywhere in the United States would have to be returned to their owners.

Senators were almost evenly divided over the compromise. A tie vote in the Senate would mean the vice president would vote to break the tie. Fillmore let it be known that he would vote in favor of it. However, President Taylor was against the compromise. The president and vice president were on opposite sides of the issue.

▲ Senator Henry Clay proposed a compromise to end debate in the Senate over the issue of slavery.

◄ As vice president, Fillmore would break any tie votes in the Senate.

A New President

★ ★ ★

In the middle of the debate over the compromise, President Taylor became seriously ill. After sitting in the hot sun at an Independence Day celebration and drinking spoiled milk, Taylor came down with severe food poisoning. He died five days later, after just sixteen months as president.

Daniel Webster was ◄ President Fillmore's secretary of state.

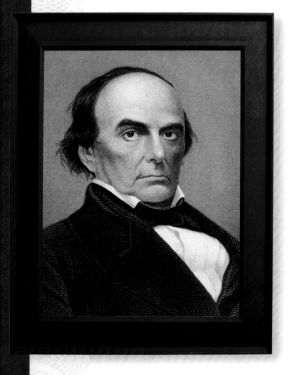

Millard Fillmore would now have to lead the nation as its new president. After learning of Taylor's death, Fillmore spent a sleepless night worrying about the challenges ahead. He took the presidential oath of office on July 10, 1850, and went right to work. His first task was to select a new **cabinet.** When Taylor died, all the members of his cabinet quit. They knew that the new president would want to choose other people. Fillmore convinced Senator Daniel Webster of

Massachusetts to be his **secretary of state** and named Kentucky governor John J. Crittenden his **attorney general.** Both supported the compromise bill. Fillmore wanted them to help him convince the Senate to pass the bill.

With Fillmore's support, Congress passed each part of the bill, which became known as the Compromise of 1850. Fillmore believed his support for the bill had helped keep the Union from falling apart.

▼ *Map illustrating the Compromise of 1850*

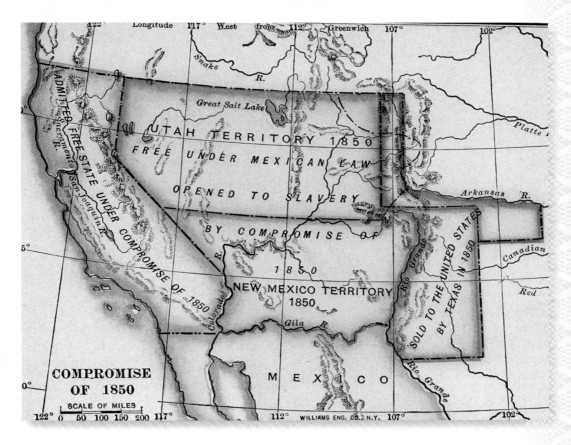

The nation was still divided, however. Northerners against slavery were outraged by the compromise's harsh **fugitive** slave law. Southern slave owners believed that they had given up too much for the bill and believed slavery was under attack. Fillmore's own Whig Party was torn apart by disagreements over slavery. It divided into Northern and Southern factions. Within a few years, the party disappeared entirely.

Henry Clay (standing) ▶ addressing the U.S. Senate on the issue of slavery, which continued to divide the nation even after the Compromise of 1850.

Fillmore believed there was little the federal government could do about slavery. "God knows that I detest slavery," he wrote. However, he claimed that any effort to limit or end slavery was against the law. "We must give [slavery] such protection as guaranteed by the Constitution," Fillmore declared. He announced that he would see to it that the fugitive slave law was strictly enforced. In a message to Congress on December 2, 1850, he declared that each state should be allowed to decide for itself about slavery.

▲ *Mary Abigail Fillmore sometimes acted as hostess for her mother at the White House.*

In the middle of the uproar over the Compromise of 1850, the Fillmores had to adjust to their new life in the White House. Abigail Fillmore had a difficult time getting used to her role as first lady. She didn't like living in Washington, and she was often in poor health. As a result, her daughter, Mary Abigail, sometimes acted as hostess at White House dinners and parties.

Abigail had been surprised to find that the White House had no library. Books had always been important to her. She had received a better education than most women of her time and was determined that the White House should have its own collection of books. She convinced Congress to grant money to buy books for the White House. Then Abigail set aside a small room on the second floor to house the collection, which became the first White House library.

The White House ▶ Library as it looks today

◀ *A wagon train
of settlers heads
west over the
Sierra Nevadas
in the 1860s.*

The United States was growing during the Fillmore
presidency. More and more people were arriving from
other countries in search of jobs and freedom. At the
same time, Americans continued to move from east
to west, settling newly acquired territories. Railroads
became an important way of transporting people and
goods across the growing country.

Railroad construction in about 1850

As president, Fillmore tried to improve the nation's transportation system. He urged Congress to pay for new and better railroads, waterways, and harbors. To Fillmore, a good transportation system was key to America's economic success.

He also tried to build American trade with other countries. Fillmore approved a plan to open trade with Japan. For more than three hundred years, Japan had mostly refused to allow trading ships from other countries into its harbors. In 1852, Commodore Matthew Perry of the U.S. Navy set sail for Japan to get the Japanese to open their doors to trade. The following year, Japan finally agreed to trade with the United States.

Fillmore also tried to protect American business interests overseas. In 1851, Hawaii was still an independent kingdom. However, some Americans hoped that one day it

▼ *Commodore Matthew Perry met the Japanese at Yokohama in 1854.*

The Hawaiian ▲
island of Kauai
in the 1800s

would be part of the United States. American ships often stopped in Hawaii to get supplies during their long trips across the Pacific. When France began to show interest in taking over the Hawaiian Islands, Fillmore had to act quickly. His secretary of state, Daniel Webster, told French leaders that the United States would not allow the French to take over Hawaii.

Later Years

★ ★ ★

Early in his term as president, Fillmore told some friends that he had no desire to run for reelection in 1852. He wanted to return to a quieter life with his family in New York. However, some Whigs convinced Fillmore to try to run for president anyway. His heart was never really in it, though, and the Whigs did not even choose him as their presidential candidate. Instead, they chose General Winfield Scott. He, in turn, lost the election to Democrat Franklin Pierce.

▼ *Franklin Pierce won the 1852 presidential election.*

Abigail Fillmore was glad to leave Washington and return to New York. She never got the chance to enjoy her return home, however. Abigail became ill with pneumonia, a disease of the lungs, at Franklin Pierce's swearing-in ceremony. By the end of the month, she was dead. A little more than a year later, Fillmore's daughter, Mary Abigail, died of cholera. Fillmore had suddenly lost two of the most important people in his life. He was sad and unsure of what to do next.

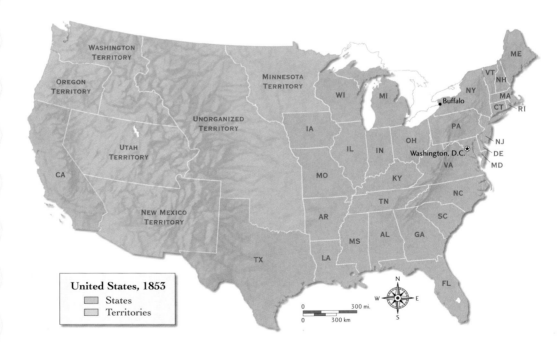

United States, 1853
States
Territories

Fillmore spent a year traveling in Europe, where he met leaders such as Queen Victoria of Great Britain. Because of his good taste and love of books, Fillmore had earned the nickname the "American Louis Philippe," after a king of France. On his trip to Europe, however, he turned down an honorary degree from famed Oxford University because it was written in Latin. No one, he said, should accept a degree he cannot read. Upon his return to the United States, Fillmore realized he was not yet ready to end his political career.

▼ *Queen Victoria was one of the world leaders Fillmore met during his travels in Europe.*

Fillmore became involved in forming a new political party. Its official name was the American Party, but everyone called it the Know-Nothing Party. It got that name because many of its members tried to keep secret the fact that they were involved with the party—they claimed to know nothing about it.

Members of the new party thought that too many people were moving to the United States from other countries. The Know-Nothings wanted

FILLMORE
AND
DONELSON

THE
UNION

FILLMORE & DONELSON

NATIONAL UNION.

"I know nothing but my Country, my whole Country, and nothing but my Country."

A campaign ribbon for the 1856 election showing running mates Millard Fillmore (left) and Andrew Jackson Donelson

to limit the number of these immigrants. They also wanted a waiting period before new citizens were allowed to vote. The party chose Fillmore as its presidential candidate in 1856, but he was defeated again. He finished behind both Republican candidate John C. Fremont and Democrat James Buchanan, the winner.

With his political career over, Fillmore grew worried about his finances. He needed to make money, but he didn't want to do any work that could be considered unworthy of a former president. He wrote, "It is a national disgrace that our presidents . . . should be cast adrift, and perhaps be compelled to keep a corner grocery [to make a living]."

▲ *Fillmore became concerned about his financial situation after his political career came to an end.*

Caroline Carmichael ▲
McIntosh became
Fillmore's second
wife in 1858 and
lived with her
husband in this
mansion in Buffalo.

Fillmore's solution was to marry a wealthy woman named Caroline Carmichael McIntosh. They married in 1858 and moved into a large mansion in Buffalo. During the next fifteen years, Fillmore and his wife were active in many local groups. Fillmore helped found the Buffalo Hospital, the Buffalo Historical Society, and the Buffalo chapter of the Society for the Prevention of Cruelty to Animals.

On February 13, 1874, Fillmore suffered a **stroke** that left him unable to move the left side of his body. Several weeks later, he suffered a second stroke. He never recovered and died in his sleep on March 8, 1874.

▼ *Fillmore's funeral was held on March 12, 1874, at Saint Paul's Cathedral in Buffalo.*

Millard Fillmore's ▼
burial site at Forest
Lawn Cemetery
in Buffalo

Today, Fillmore is one of the most overlooked presidents. He served as president for just over two and a half years and was never elected by voters. However, his presidency came during an important time in the nation's history. When Fillmore was president, the United States was becoming increasingly divided between free states and slave states. Like other presidents of the 1850s, he looked for ways to keep the Union together.

Despite his best efforts, Fillmore was unable to prevent the arrival of the long and bloody Civil War, which settled the divisive slavery issue once and for all.

GLOSSARY

★ ★ ★

attorney general—a state or nation's top lawyer

cabinet—a president's group of advisers who are heads of departments

campaign—an organized effort to win an election

candidate—someone running for office in an election

compromise—an agreement that is reached by both sides giving up part of what they want

comptroller—a person in charge of government finances

convention—a large meeting during which a political party chooses its candidates

debates—formal arguments

free states—states that did not allow slavery in the years before the Civil War

fugitive—runaway

gavel—a hammer used to get attention

legislature—the part of government that makes or changes laws

presiding—being in charge

secretary of state—the president's leading adviser in dealing with other countries

slave states—states that allowed slavery in the years before the Civil War

stroke—a problem in the brain causing a sudden loss of the ability to feel or move

MILLARD FILLMORE'S LIFE AT A GLANCE

★ ★ ★

PERSONAL

Nickname:	The American Louis Philippe
Born:	January 7, 1800
Birthplace:	Locke (now Summerhill), New York
Father's name:	Nathaniel Fillmore
Mother's name:	Phoebe Millard Fillmore
Education:	Studied law under Judge Walter Wood
Wives' names:	Abigail Powers Fillmore (1798–1853); Caroline Carmichael McIntosh Fillmore (1813–1881)
Married:	February 5, 1826; February 10, 1858
Children:	Millard Powers Fillmore (1828–1889); Mary Abigail Fillmore (1832–1854)
Died:	March 8, 1874, in Buffalo, New York
Buried:	Forest Lawn Cemetery in Buffalo, New York

PUBLIC

Occupation before presidency:	Lawyer, politician
Occupation after presidency:	Lawyer
Military service:	None
Other government positions:	Member of the New York State Assembly; representative from New York in the U.S. House of Representatives; New York state comptroller; vice president
Political parties:	Anti-Mason, Whig, and Know-Nothing
Vice president:	None
Dates in office:	July 10, 1850–March 4, 1853
Presidential opponents:	James Buchanan (Democrat), John C. Fremont (Republican), 1856
Number of votes (Electoral College):	871,731 of 4,044,618 (8 of 296), 1856
Writings:	None

Millard Fillmore's Cabinet

Secretary of state:
John M. Clayton (1850)
Daniel Webster (1850–1852)
Edward Everett (1852–1853)

Secretary of the treasury:
William M. Meredith (1850)
Thomas Corwin (1850–1853)

Secretary of war:
George W. Crawford (1850)
Charles M. Conrad (1850–1853)

Attorney general:
Reverdy Johnson (1850)
John J. Crittenden (1850–1853)

Postmaster general:
Jacob Collamer (1850)
Nathan K. Hall (1850–1852)
Samuel D. Hubbard (1852–1853)

Secretary of the navy:
William B. Preston (1850)
William A. Graham (1850–1852)
John P. Kennedy (1852–1853)

Secretary of the interior:
Thomas Ewing (1850)
Thomas M. T. McKennan (1850)
Alexander H. H. Stuart (1850–1853)

MILLARD FILLMORE'S LIFE AND TIMES

★ ★ ★

FILLMORE'S LIFE

January 7, Fillmore **1800**
is born to Phoebe
and Nathaniel
Fillmore (below) in
Locke, New York

WORLD EVENTS

1800

1801   Ultraviolet radiation
is discovered

1805   General anesthesia is
first used in surgery

1807   Robert Fulton's
Clermont (below) is
the first reliable
steamship to travel
between New York
City and Albany

1809   American poet and
short-story writer
Edgar Allen Poe is
born in Boston

FILLMORE'S LIFE

WORLD EVENTS

1810

1810   Bernardo O'Higgins (right) leads Chile in its fight for independence from Spain

1812–
1814   The United States and Britain fight the War of 1812

1814–
1815   European states meet in Vienna, Austria, to redraw national borders after the conclusion of the Napoleonic Wars

Attends New   1819
Hope Academy

1820

1820   Susan B. Anthony (right), a leader of the American woman suffrage movement, is born

1821   Central American countries gain independence from Spain

Becomes a lawyer   1823

1823   Mexico becomes a republic

FILLMORE'S LIFE

Marries Abigail Powers (above)	1826
Joins the Anti-Masonic movement	
Elected to the New York state legislature	1828
Elected to the U.S. House of Representatives	1832

WORLD EVENTS

1825	Powered by a steam engine, England's first public railroad begins operation
1826	The first photograph is taken by Joseph Niépce, a French physicist
1827	Modern-day matches are invented by coating the end of a wooden stick with phosphorus
1829	The first practical sewing machine is invented by French tailor Barthélemy Thimonnier (below)

1830

1833	Great Britain abolishes slavery

FILLMORE'S LIFE		WORLD EVENTS	
		1836	Texans defeat Mexican troops at San Jacinto after a deadly battle at the Alamo (right) 
Returns to the U.S. House of Representatives	1837	1837	American banker J. P. Morgan is born
	1840	1840	Auguste Rodin, famous sculptor of *The Thinker* (right), is born 
Runs for governor of New York, but loses	1844		
Becomes a founder and the first chancellor of the University of Buffalo	1846		
Elected New York state comptroller	1847		
Elected vice president	1848	1848	*The Communist Manifesto,* by German writer Karl Marx (right), is widely distributed 

FILLMORE'S LIFE			WORLD EVENTS	
July 10, becomes president when President Zachary Taylor dies	1850	1850	1850	Jeans are invented by Levi Strauss, a German who came to America during the gold rush
Congress passes the Compromise of 1850				

Sends Commodore Matthew C. Perry to Japan to open trade (below)	1852	1852	American Harriet Beecher Stowe (above) publishes *Uncle Tom's Cabin*

Runs for president as the candidate of the Know-Nothing Party — 1856

FILLMORE'S LIFE

Marries Caroline Carmichael McIntosh (below) — 1858

Elected first president of the Buffalo Historical Society, which he helped establish — 1862

Founds the Buffalo chapter of the Society for the Prevention of Cruelty to Animals — 1873

March 8, dies at age 74 — 1874

WORLD EVENTS

1858 — English scientist Charles Darwin (below) presents his theory of evolution

1860 — Austrian composer Gustav Mahler is born in Kalischt (now in Austria)

1868 — Louisa May Alcott publishes *Little Women*

1869 — The transcontinental railroad across the United States is completed (below)

1860

1870

UNDERSTANDING MILLARD FILLMORE AND HIS PRESIDENCY

★ ★ ★

IN THE LIBRARY

Cleveland, Will, and Mark Alvarez. *Yo, Millard Fillmore (And All Those Other Presidents You Don't Know)*. Brookfield, Conn.: Millbrook Press, 1997.

Joseph, Paul. *Millard Fillmore*. Minneapolis: Abdo & Daughters, 2000.

Souter, Gerry, and Janet Souter. *Millard Fillmore: Our 13th President*. Chanhassen, Minn.: The Child's World, 2002.

ON THE WEB

For more information on this topic, use FactHound.

1. Go to *www.facthound.com*
2. Type in this book ID: 0756502616
3. Click on the *Fetch It* button.

FactHound will find the best Web sites for you.

FILLMORE HISTORIC SITES
ACROSS THE COUNTRY

The Millard Fillmore House
24 Shearer Avenue
East Aurora, NY 14052
716/652-8875
To visit Fillmore's house and learn
more about how people lived in
1826, the year it was built

Millard Fillmore Log Cabin
Fillmore Glen State Park
Moravia, NY 13118
315/497-0131
To see a replica of the log cabin
where Fillmore was born

Fillmore's Gravesite
Forest Lawn Cemetery
1411 Delaware Avenue
Buffalo, NY 14209
716/885-1600
To visit Fillmore's burial place

THE U.S. PRESIDENTS
(Years in Office)

★ ★ ★

1. **George Washington**
(March 4, 1789-March 3, 1797)
2. **John Adams**
(March 4, 1797-March 3, 1801)
3. **Thomas Jefferson**
(March 4, 1801-March 3, 1809)
4. **James Madison**
(March 4, 1809-March 3, 1817)
5. **James Monroe**
(March 4, 1817-March 3, 1825)
6. **John Quincy Adams**
(March 4, 1825-March 3, 1829)
7. **Andrew Jackson**
(March 4, 1829-March 3, 1837)
8. **Martin Van Buren**
(March 4, 1837-March 3, 1841)
9. **William Henry Harrison**
(March 6, 1841-April 4, 1841)
10. **John Tyler**
(April 6, 1841-March 3, 1845)
11. **James K. Polk**
(March 4, 1845-March 3, 1849)
12. **Zachary Taylor**
(March 5, 1849-July 9, 1850)
13. Millard Fillmore
(July 10, 1850-March 3, 1853)
14. **Franklin Pierce**
(March 4, 1853-March 3, 1857)
15. **James Buchanan**
(March 4, 1857-March 3, 1861)
16. **Abraham Lincoln**
(March 4, 1861-April 15, 1865)
17. **Andrew Johnson**
(April 15, 1865-March 3, 1869)

18. **Ulysses S. Grant**
(March 4, 1869-March 3, 1877)
19. **Rutherford B. Hayes**
(March 4, 1877-March 3, 1881)
20. **James Garfield**
(March 4, 1881-Sept 19, 1881)
21. **Chester Arthur**
(Sept 20, 1881-March 3, 1885)
22. **Grover Cleveland**
(March 4, 1885-March 3, 1889)
23. **Benjamin Harrison**
(March 4, 1889-March 3, 1893)
24. **Grover Cleveland**
(March 4, 1893-March 3, 1897)
25. **William McKinley**
(March 4, 1897-
September 14, 1901)
26. **Theodore Roosevelt**
(September 14, 1901-
March 3, 1909)
27. **William Howard Taft**
(March 4, 1909-March 3, 1913)
28. **Woodrow Wilson**
(March 4, 1913-March 3, 1921)
29. **Warren G. Harding**
(March 4, 1921-August 2, 1923)
30. **Calvin Coolidge**
(August 3, 1923-March 3, 1929)
31. **Herbert Hoover**
(March 4, 1929-March 3, 1933)
32. **Franklin D. Roosevelt**
(March 4, 1933-April 12, 1945)

33. **Harry S. Truman**
(April 12, 1945-
January 20, 1953)
34. **Dwight D. Eisenhower**
(January 20, 1953-
January 20, 1961)
35. **John F. Kennedy**
(January 20, 1961-
November 22, 1963)
36. **Lyndon B. Johnson**
(November 22, 1963-
January 20, 1969)
37. **Richard M. Nixon**
(January 20, 1969-
August 9, 1974)
38. **Gerald R. Ford**
(August 9, 1974-
January 20, 1977)
39. **James Earl Carter**
(January 20, 1977-
January 20, 1981)
40. **Ronald Reagan**
(January 20, 1981-
January 20, 1989)
41. **George H. W. Bush**
(January 20, 1989-
January 20, 1993)
42. **William Jefferson Clinton**
(January 20, 1993-
January 20, 2001)
43. **George W. Bush**
(January 20, 2001-)

INDEX

★ ★ ★

Index

ABOUT THE AUTHOR

Andrew Santella writes for magazines and newspapers, including *GQ* and the *New York Times Book Review.* He is the author of a number of books for young readers. He lives outside Chicago, with his wife and son.